MW00510772

Copycat Recipes

Made Easy

Amazing Copycat Cookbook For Everyone. Sit at

Home and Cook like your Favorite Restaurant

and Enjoy Every day

Ashlee Reed

Disclaimer Notice:

Please note the information contained within this document is for educational and entertainment purposes only. All effort has been executed to present accurate, up to date, and reliable, complete information. No warranties of any kind are declared or implied. Readers acknowledge that the author is not engaging in the rendering of legal, financial, medical or professional advice. The content within this book has been derived from various sources. Please consult a licensed professional before attempting any techniques outlined in this book.

By reading this document, the reader agrees that under no circumstances is the author responsible for any losses, direct or indirect, which are incurred as a result of the use of information contained within this document, including, but not limited to, errors, omissions, or inaccuracies.

Table Of Content

Introduction

Thank You For Purchasing **Copycat Recipes Made Easy: Amazing Copycat Cookbook For Everyone. Sit at Home and Cook like your Favorite Restaurant and Enjoy Every day**

You can easily cook your favorite recipes with a little practice and patience. You would just want to cook the basic formula and start adding what you think would make the flavor of the recipe better after a while. But if you've ever badly prepared food of this kind on your own, it is not impossible! With a few and simple tricks and tips, you can also cook quality cuisine in your own kitchen. These tricks may not seem so strong on their own but can transform how you prepare and produce food when they are all used together.

Breakfast

Paris' Crepes

Preparation Time: 35 minutes

Cooking Time: 20 minutes

Servings: 4

Ingredients:

- 1 cup flour

- 2 eggs

- 1 tablespoon sugar

- ¼ tablespoon kosher salt

- 2 cups milk (whole)

- 1 ½ tablespoon butter

- Fresh fruits of your choice (for serving)

- Powdered sugar (for serving)

Directions:

1. Combine and mix the flour together with sugar, and salt in a mixing bowl. Make a well in the center and start adding the eggs. Pour milk in the flour mix and whisk properly until combined. Allow the batter to sit at room temperature for twenty minutes.

2.   Take a small skillet and heat the butter in it. Add one-fourth cup batter to the skillet. Swirl the skillet for coating properly.

3.   Cook the crepes for two minutes and flip. Cook for 1 more minute. Repeat the same with the remaining batter.

4.   Serve the hot crepes with powdered sugar and fruits from the top. Add chocolate syrup to the crepes if you want to.

Nutrition:

- Calories: 162

- Protein: 3.2g

- Carbs: 13g

- Fat: 4.6g

- Sugar: 0.9g

Cracker Barrel's Lemon Pepper Trout

Preparation Time: 10 minutes

Cooking Time: 15 minutes

Servings: 4–5

Ingredients:

- 6 (4-ounce) trout fillets

- 3 tablespoons butter, melted

- 2 medium lemons, thinly sliced

- 2 tablespoons lemon juice

- Sauce

- 3 tablespoons butter

- ¼ teaspoon pepper

- 2 tablespoons lemon juice

Directions:

In a saucepan, it melts the butter over low warmness and enables it to cook until it starts to brown. Add the pepper and lemon juice. Brush the fish fillets with melted butter. Lay lemon slices on top of each.

If cooking on a grill, use a wire grilling basket sprayed with nonstick cooking spray. Grill for about 10 minutes or until the fish flakes effortlessly with a fork. Alternatively, you can bake in a 350°F oven for 10–15 minutes. Transfer to a serving platter and top with extra lemon slices.

Serve with the butter lemon sauce you made.

Nutrition:

- Calories: 242.8

- Fat: 6.6g,

- Carbs: 38.4g

- Sugars: 3g

- Protein: 8.4g

Cracker Barrel's Mushroom Swiss Chopped Steak

Preparation Time: 10 minutes

Cooking Time: 30 minutes

Servings: 4

Ingredients:

- 1-pound floor sirloin, fashioned into four patties

- 1 tablespoon butter

- Salt to taste

- Pepper to taste

- 4 slices Swiss cheese

- ¼ small onion, sliced

- 1-pound mushrooms, sliced

- 1 (14 ½-ounce) can beef gravy (or equal package)

Directions:

1.   Season the sirloin patties with salt and pepper, then cook to the favored temperature. You can grill, broil, fry, or

even bake the ground meat; the choice is yours. Put the cooked patties to a plate and top everyone with a slice of Swiss cheese.

2.	Sauté the mushroom and onion in a large pan. Add the red meat gravy. Top each patty with the onion, mushroom, and pork gravy mixture.

Nutrition:

- Calories: 150
- Fat: 4.2g
- Carbs: 40g
- Sugars: 1g
- Protein: 9g

Paris' Coq Au Vin

Preparation Time: 30 minutes

Cooking Time: 1 hour

Servings: 6

Ingredients:

- 3 pounds chicken drumsticks and thighs
- 2 tablespoons black pepper (ground)
- 6 bacon strips (cut in pieces of one inch)
- 8 ounces baby Bella mushrooms (sliced)
- 5 ounces onions (peeled)
- 1 carrot (chopped)
- 2 garlic cloves (minced)
- 1 tablespoon tomato paste
- 2 tablespoons flour
- 2 cups red wine
- 1 cup chicken stock
- 1 tablespoon brandy
- 1 bunch of thyme
- 3 tablespoons butter

- Parsley (chopped, for garnishing)

Directions:

1. Preheat your oven to 180°C.

2. Season the chicken with pepper and salt.

3. Take a skillet and cook the bacon until crispy. Cook for about eight minutes. Remove the bacon and keep aside.

4. Cook the chicken in the pot for 5 minutes on each side. Remove the chicken and keep aside.

5. Combine the onions, carrots, and mushrooms to the pot. Cook for 5 minutes until golden. Add the garlic and tomato paste. Give it a stir for coating the veggies. Add flour to the mixture and stir.

6. Slowly add the red wine, brandy, and chicken stock to the mixture. Return the cooked chicken to the pot along with half of the cooked bacon. Season with pepper and salt and add thyme. Boil the mixture.

7. When it is starting to boil, cover the pot and put it in the oven. Cook until the chicken gets evenly cooked for thirty minutes. Remove the chicken.

8.   Return the mixture pot to the stove and add butter to it. Simmer the mixture for ten minutes until the sauce thickens.

9.   Serve the chicken with sauce from the top. Add remaining bacon from the top along with parsley.

Nutrition:

- Calories: 265

- Protein: 32g

- Carbs: 7.3g

- Fat: 7.8g

- Sugar: 2.1g

Cracker Barrel's Hash Brown Casserole

Preparation Time: 10 minutes

Cooking Time: 45 minutes

Servings: 4–6

Ingredients:

- 1 (30-ounce) bag frozen hash browns, thawed

- ½ cup butter, melted

- 1 can cream of fowl soup

- 1 small onion, chopped

- 1-pound cheddar cheese, shredded (divided)

- 1 teaspoon salt

- ½ teaspoon black pepper

- 1 cup butter cream

Directions:

1.   Preheat oven to 350°F.

2.   Prepare a baking dish either by using greasing the aspects or spraying with nonstick cooking spray.

3.   Mix the onion, cream of hen soup, pepper, and all however 1 cup the shredded cheese in a massive bowl. When

combined, combine in the bitter cream until it is well incorporated.

4.   Add the melted butter and hash browns. Stir to combine. Pour into the greased baking dish.

5.   Bake for forty-five minutes or till bubbly, then sprinkle the last cheese on top and bake again in 5–10 minutes or until the cheese is melted.

Nutrition:

- Calories: 112

- Fat: 17g

- Carbs: 50g

- Protein: 7g

Cracker Barrel's Buttermilk Pancakes

Preparation Time: 5 minutes

Cooking Time: 15 minutes

Servings: 6

Ingredients:

- 2 cups un-sifted flour
- 2 teaspoons baking soda
- 1 teaspoon salt
- 3 tablespoons sugar
- 2 eggs
- 2⅓ cups low-fat buttermilk
- Butter for cooking

Directions:

1. Preheat a grill or massive skillet to 350°F.

2. Place a stick of butter after the skillet; you will butter it earlier than making ready every pancake.

3. In a medium bowl, put the eggs and buttermilk and whisk till they are properly combined. Whisk in the flour,

baking soda, sugar, and salt. Whisk wholly till nicely combined.

4.   Prepare the skillet with the aid of rubbing the butter in a circle in the center, then add about ½ cup batter. Spread the batter till its varieties an even circle.

5.   When the pancake surface turns bubbly, flip and cook on the different aspects until you can't see moist spots on the sides.

6.   Repeat with the last batter, making sure to butter the skillet earlier than you start each pancake.

7.   Serve with your favorite syrup or fruit.

Nutrition:

- Calories: 80
- Fat: 4g
- Carbs: 20g
- Sugars 2g
- Protein: 15g

Main

Maggiano's Little Italy's Spinach and Artichoke Al Forno

Preparation Time: 20 minutes

Cooking Time: 20 minutes

Servings: 15

Ingredients:

- ½ cup sliced scallions

- 2 cups canned artichokes (drained and rinsed)

- 1 cup heavy cream

- 2 cups shredded Asiago cheese

- 3 tablespoons olive oil

- 2 cups sautéed spinach (drained and sliced)

- Pepper and salt to taste

- 1 tablespoon grated parmesan cheese

- ¼ cup chopped sun-dried tomatoes

Directions:

1. Preheat your oven to 350°F.

2.   Put the scallions, heavy cream, spinach, Asiago cheese, olive oil, tomatoes, and artichokes in a bowl, then put some pepper and salt to taste.

3.   Transfer the mixture into a greased oven friendly bowl, then top the mixture with the shredded parmesan cheese. Place the bowl in the middle tier of the oven and bake for 20 minutes at 350°F. Remove from the oven. Serve with slices Italian bread.

Nutrition:

- Calories: 150

- Fat: 20g

- Carbs: 50g

- Protein: 15g

Steak and Ale's Burgundy Mushrooms

Preparation Time: 10 minutes

Cooking Time: 20 minutes

Servings: 3

Ingredients:

- ¼ pounds mushrooms

- 2 quarts water

- ¼ cup lemon juice

- 4 tablespoons margarine

- ¾ cup yellow onions, diced

- ½ cup Burgundy

- 1 tablespoon hamburger bouillon granules

- ¼ teaspoon garlic powder

- ⅓ teaspoon ground white pepper

Directions:

1.   Clean and dry the mushrooms. Join water and lemon juice in a secured saucepan. Bring to a bubble. In another pot,

liquefy margarine and sauté onions until smooth (around 5 minutes).

2.   In a bowl, add flavors and bouillon to Burgundy. Rush until bouillon is broken up. Add wine blend to onions. Stew over medium warmth around 10 minutes (until the liquor has vanished). Expel from heat. Add mushrooms to bubbling lemon water. Come back to the bubble. Expel whitened mushrooms from heat and altogether channel. Add mushrooms to wine sauce and mix until mixed.

Nutrition:

1.   Calories: 178

2.   Fat: 15g

3.   Carbs: 50g

4.   Sugars: 8g

5.   Protein: 9g

Maggiano's Little Italy's Steamed Mussels

Preparation Time: 20 minutes

Cooking Time: 10 minutes

Servings: 2

Ingredients:

- 1 tablespoon freshly squeezed lemon juice

- 20 mussels

- ½ teaspoon chopped basil

- 2 tablespoons cannellini beans

- ¾ cup chicken stock

- ½ tablespoon of minced garlic

- ½ cup white wine

- 2 tablespoons sun-dried tomatoes

- 2 tablespoons butter

- ½ tablespoon chopped parsley

- Salt and pepper

Directions:

1.   Combine the garlic and wine in a pan over medium heat.

2.   Once hot, add the mussels and cook covered on high until the mussels open, about 5 minutes.

3.   Put in the remaining ingredients, stir and allow to simmer over medium heat for 2-3 minutes. Put some pepper and salt to taste.

4.   Serve the mussels in a bowl, drizzle with sauce, and then serve with 2-3 slices garlic toast.

Nutrition:

- Calories: 178

- Fat: 15g

- Carbs: 50g

- Sugars: 8g

- Protein: 9g

Maggiano's Little Italy's Veal Marsala

Preparation Time: 10 minutes

Cooking Time: 20 minutes

Servings: 4

Ingredients:

- ¾ cup low sodium chicken broth

- 8 veal cutlets

- 2 ounces mixed mushrooms (sliced)

- Salt and pepper to taste

- ½ cup sweet Marsala

- 1 shallot (sliced)

- 3 tablespoons unsalted butter

- 1 tablespoon chopped fresh rosemary leaves

- 3 cloves garlic (crushed)

- 3 tablespoons olive oil

Directions:

1. Season salt and pepper all over the veal cutlets.

2. Heat two tablespoons of oil and butter in a large skillet over medium heat, add veal cutlets. Cook each side for 2-3 minutes or until browned, then remove and keep warm until ready to use.

3.   Heat the oil in the skillet, add garlic and sauté until soft and fragrant, and then add the mushrooms.

4.   Add some pepper and salt to season, then add the Marsala and cook for 2-3 minutes.

5.   Add the rosemary leaves and broth, stir and cook for 4 minutes, then add the cutlets and cook for 1-2 minutes, pouring the sauce over the veal while stirring.

6.   Stir in the last tablespoon of butter and cook for a minute or until the butter has completely melted.

7.   Put the cutlets on plates and scoop the sauce over them.

Nutrition:

•   Calories: 80

•   Fat: 4g

•   Carbs: 20g

•   Sugars: 2g

•   Protein: 15g

Sbarro's Rigatoni Ala Vodka

Preparation Time: 15 minutes

Cooking Time: 30 minutes

Servings: 4

Ingredients:

- 2 lbs. rigatoni

- 24 ounces canned pureed tomatoes (plain)

- 2 tablespoons olive oil

- 2 cloves new garlic, minced

- ½ teaspoon split red pepper

- 1 tablespoon salt

- ½ teaspoon dark pepper

- 1 teaspoon dried basil

- ½ quart substantial cream

- ½ ounces vodka

- 1 ounces ground Romano Cheese

- 1 ounces bacon bits

- ½ ounces Italian parsley slashed

Directions:

1. In a medium sauce skillet, heat oil until hot. Include garlic and sauté until brilliant earthy colored. Include pureed

tomatoes, salt, red pepper, dark pepper, and basil. Cook over medium warmth, mixing sometimes until completely warmed. Include substantial cream and vodka. Mix to blend and cook for a while.

2.   Bubble rigatoni (don't overcook). In a blending bowl, join depleted pasta with cream sauce. Blend altogether. Place it to a bowl and top with ground cheddar, bacon, and parsley. Serve right away.

Nutrition:

- Calories: 100
- Fat: 3g
- Carbs: 21g
- Sugars: 10g
- Protein: 5g

Maggiano's Little Italy's Whole Roasted Chicken

Preparation Time: 25 minutes

Cooking Time: 1 hour

Servings: 6

Ingredients:

- Salt and pepper to taste
- 1 whole chicken (washed and dried with a paper towel)
- 2 tablespoons lemon zest
- ½ cup softened butter
- 2 tablespoons olive oil
- 4 lemon wedges
- ¼ cup sliced onions
- ¼ cup chopped fresh rosemary leaves
- 2 ½ tablespoons freshly squeezed lemon juice
- 3 cloves garlic (minced)

Directions:

1. Preheat your oven to 425°F.

2.   Put the olive oil, butter, lemon zest, garlic, and rosemary into a medium bowl, stir until well combined, then set aside.

3.   Put some pepper and salt all over the chicken and inside the cavity.

4.   Brush a generous amount of the butter mixture into the chicken, making sure it is properly coated.

5.   Drizzle the lemon juice all over the chicken and stuff with chopped rosemary, two lemon wedges, and sliced onions.

6.   Place the chicken on the pan and put into the oven. Bake for 40-45 minutes, remove from the oven and baste with more of the butter mixture.

7.   Bake the chicken in the oven for another 10-15 minutes or until golden brown.

8.   Remove the chicken from the oven and let it cool before serving.

Nutrition:

- Calories: 178

- Fat: 24g

- Carbs: 123g

- Sugars: 15g
- Protein: 27g

SIDES & APPETIZER

Moe's Southwestern Grill's Taco Pie

Preparation Time: 10 minutes

Cooking Time: 35 minutes

Servings: 4–6

Ingredients:

- 1 ½ cups crushed tortilla chips
- 2 teaspoons taco seasoning
- 3 tablespoons butter, melted
- 3 cups leftover taco beef
- 1 ½ cups refried beans
- 1 cup spicy salsa
- 1 cup grated cheddar cheese
- Cherry tomatoes, halved

Toppings:

- Salsa
- Sour cream or crema
- Chopped salad

Directions:

1.   Preheat the oven to 450°F.

2.   In a mixing bowl, combine the crushed tortilla chips, taco seasoning, and melted butter. Mix well and press the crust into a 9-inch pie plate. Bake for 10 minutes.

3.   Reduce the oven temperature to 375°F.

4.   Spoon the taco beef into the crust and spread the refried beans on it. Layer the salsa on top, and then the grated cheddar. Scatter the tomatoes on top.

5.   Bake for 20 minutes, switching to broil in the final few minutes to ensure the cheese is melted and lightly browned.

6.   Let the pie cool down before slicing. Serve with favorite toppings.

Nutrition:

•   Calories: 140

•   Fat: 8g

•   Carbs: 30

•   Sugars: 10g

•   Protein: 25g

Mexican's Shrimp Taco Bites

Preparation Time: 10 minutes

Cooking Time: 1 minute

Serving: 24

Ingredients:

- 24 wonton wrappers

- Oil to coat

- Guacamole

Shrimp:

- ½ pound shrimp, peeled and deveined

- 1 lime, juiced

- 2 Tablespoons cilantro, coarsely chopped

- ¼ cup olive oil

- ½ teaspoon sea salt

- ½ teaspoon black pepper

- ¼ teaspoon cayenne

Cabbage slaw:

- ¼ cup mayonnaise

- 1 ½ Tablespoons lime juice

- ¼ teaspoon lime zest (optional)

- 2 Tablespoons cilantro

- 1 teaspoon jalapeños, chopped

- Pinch of sea salt

- 2 cups red cabbage, shredded

Toppings:

- Jalapeno slices

- Cotija cheese

- Cilantro leaves

Directions:

1. Mix the lime juice, shrimp, and cilantro together with the olive oils, salt, and pepper to taste and cayenne. Marinade it for 15-20 minutes.

2. Preheat your oven to 350°F.

3. Put some wonton wrapper on the mini muffin tin and gently push down the middle to line the cup with wonton. Brush the wrappers with olive oil then bake it for 10 minutes until it turns golden brown and set aside.

4.   In the meantime, whisk the mayonnaise, zest, lime juice, salt, and jalapenos together and add the cabbage to the mixture.

5.   Heat a pan in medium-high heat then add the shrimp and marinade. Let it cook for 1-2 minutes each side. Once done, set it aside to let it cool slightly. Then, slice the shrimps into halves of thirds and put it into the cabbage slaw.

6.   Put one teaspoon on guacamole on the bottom of each wonton cup. Put in some of the shrimp mixture and cabbage slaw. Do this for all of the cups. Top them with cilantro, jalapeno slices, and cotija cheese.

Nutrition:

- Calories: 140

- Fat: 8g

- Carbs: 30

- Sugars: 10g

- Protein: 25g

Pei Wei's Vietnamese Chicken Salad Spring Roll

Preparation Time: 10 minutes

Cooking Time: 1 minute

Serving: 4-6

Ingredients:

- Salad

- Rice Wrappers

- Green leaf lettuce like Boston Bibb lettuce

- Napa cabbage, shredded

- Green onions, chopped

- Mint, chopped

- Carrots, cut into 1-inch matchsticks

- Peanuts

- Chicken, diced and cooked, about 6 chicken tenders drizzled with soy sauce, honey, garlic powder, and red pepper flakes

- Lime dressing

- 2 tablespoons lime juice, about 1 lime

- 1½ teaspoons water

- 1 tablespoon sugar

- 1 teaspoon salt

- Dash of pepper

- 3 tablespoons oil

- Peanut dipping sauce

- 2 tablespoons soy sauce

- 1 tablespoon rice wine vinegar

- 2 tablespoons brown sugar

- ¼ cup peanut butter

- 1 teaspoon chipotle Tabasco

- 1 teaspoon honey

- 1 teaspoon sweet chili sauce

- 1 teaspoon lime vinaigrette

Directions:

1.   In a large bowl, mix all of the salad ingredients except for the rice wrappers and lettuce.

2.   Place the rice wrappers in warm water for about 1 minute to soften.

3.   Transfer the wrappers to a plate and top each with 2 pieces of lettuce.

4.   Top the lettuce with the salad mixture and drizzle with the lime dressing. Fold the wrapper by tucking in the ends and then rolling.

5.   Serve with lime dressing and peanut dipping sauce.

Nutrition:

- Calories: 80

- Fat: 4g

- Carbs: 20g

- Sugars: 2g

- Protein: 15g

SEAFOOD, PUOLTRY & BEEF

PF Chang's Beef A La Sichuan

Preparation Time: 20 minutes

Cooking Time: 10 minutes

Servings: 4–6

Ingredients:

- Stir-fry

- 1 pound flank steak or sirloin, sliced thin

- 4 medium celery ribs

- 2 medium carrots

- 1 green onion

- ¼ cup peanut oil or canola oil

- ¼ cup cornstarch

- ½ teaspoon red pepper flakes

- 1½ teaspoons sesame oil

Sauce:

- 3 tablespoons soy sauce

- 2 tablespoons hoisin sauce

- 1 tablespoon garlic and red chili paste

- ½ teaspoon Chinese hot mustard

- 1 teaspoon rice wine vinegar

- ½ teaspoon chili oil

- 2 teaspoons brown sugar

- 1 teaspoon garlic, minced

- ½ teaspoon fresh ginger, minced

- ½ teaspoon red pepper flakes

Directions:

1.   Mix all of the ingredients for the sauce in a mixing bowl. Set aside.

2.   Slice the carrots and celery as thinly as possible and set aside.

3.   Sprinkle the beef with the cornstarch in a bowl. Make sure every piece is coated. Allow to sit for 10 minutes.

4.   Put oil in a skillet or work over medium-high heat and cook the beef until crispy, about 4–5 minutes. When done, remove beef from the oil to a paper-towel-lined plate to drain.

5.   Discard any oil remaining in the skillet.

6.   Put some of the sesame oil to the same skillet and heat over high heat. Add the celery, stir and cook for about 1

minute. Add the crushed red pepper and stir. Add the carrots, cooking and stirring for another 30 seconds.

7.   Add the beef and green onions and stir, then pour the sauce into the skillet and bring to a boil. Let it cook for a minute, then serve over rice.

Nutrition:

- Calories: 112
- Fat: 17
- Carbs: 50g
- Sugars: 5g
- Protein: 7g

Cracker Barrel's Broccoli Cheddar Chicken

Preparation Time: 10 minutes

Cooking Time: 45 minutes

Servings: 4

Ingredients:

- 4 skinless chicken breasts
- 1 cup milk
- 1 cup Ritz-style crackers, crushed
- 1 can condensed cheddar cheese soup
- ½ pound frozen broccoli
- 6 ounces cheddar cheese, shredded
- ½ teaspoon salt
- ½ teaspoon pepper

Directions:

1. Preheat the oven to 350°F.

2. Whisk the milk and cheddar cheese soup together in a mixing bowl.

3.   Prepare a baking dish by greasing the sides, then lay the chicken in the bottom and season with the salt and pepper.

4.   Put the soup mixture on the chicken, then top with the crackers, broccoli, and shredded cheese. Bake for 45 minutes.

Nutrition:

- Calories: 150

- Fat: 4.2g

- Carbs: 40g

- Sugars: 1g

- Protein: 9g

Red Lobster's Classic BBQ Chicken

Preparation time: 5 minutes

Cooking time: 1 hour 45 minutes

Servings: 4–6

Ingredients:

- 4 pounds chicken
- Salt
- Olive oil
- 1 cup barbecue sauce

Directions:

1. Put some olive oil and salt all over the chicken.

2. In the meanwhile, preheat the griddle with high heat.

3. Grill the chicken skin side for 10 minutes.

4. Cover the chicken with foil and grill for 30 minutes in low heat.

5. Put some barbecue sauce all over the chicken.

6. Cook the chicken for another 20 minutes.

7. Baste, cover and cook again for 30 minutes.

8.   You will know that the chicken is ready when the internal temperature of the chicken pieces is 165°F and juices run clear.

9.   Baste with more barbecue sauce to serve!

Nutrition:

- Calories: 539

- Fat: 11.6g

- Carbs: 15.1g

- Sugar: 0.3g

- Protein: 87.6g

Red Lobster's Crab-Stuffed Mushrooms

Preparation Time: 10 minutes

Cooking Time: 20 minutes

Servings: 6

Ingredients:

- 1 lb. white mushrooms

- ¼ cup celery

- 2 tablespoon onion

- 2 tablespoon red bell pepper

- 5 lb. crab claw meat

- ½ cup shredded cheddar cheese

- 2 cups crushed oyster crackers

- .¼ teaspoons Salt & freshly cracked black pepper

- ½ teaspoons Old Bay Seasoning

- ¼ teaspoons garlic powder

- 1 egg

- 6 slices white cheddar cheese

Directions:

1. Warm the oven at 400° Fahrenheit.

2.   Finely chop and sauté the onions, celery, and peppers for two minutes. Transfer it in a bowl and put in the fridge.

3.   Rinse the mushrooms and remove the stems (discard half of them). Combine them with the veggies, chopped stems (if desired), rest of the fixings, except for the cheese slices.

4.   Place the mushrooms into baking dishes. Put one teaspoon of the mixture into each cup and sprinkle with cheese to bake.

5.   Bake them until lightly browned (12–15 minutes).

Nutrition:

- Calories: 115

- Fat: 14g

- Carbs: 78g

- Sugars: 9g

- Protein: 8g

Panda Express's Copycat Beef and Broccoli

Preparation Time: 30 minutes

Cooking Time: 15 minutes

Servings: 4

Ingredients:

- 2 tablespoons cornstarch, divided
- 3 tablespoons Chinese rice wine, divided
- 1 pound flank steak, cut thinly against the grain
- 1 pound broccoli florets
- 2 tablespoons oyster sauce
- 2 tablespoons water
- 1 tablespoon brown sugar
- 1 tablespoon soy sauce
- 1 tablespoon cornstarch
- 2 tablespoons canola oil
- ¼ teaspoon sesame oil
- 1 teaspoon ginger, finely chopped
- 2 cloves garlic, finely chopped

- 2 teaspoons sesame seeds

Directions:

1. In a plastic bag, put 1 tablespoon cornstarch and 2 tablespoons Chinese rice wine. Place beef inside and seal tightly. Massage bag to fully coat beef. Marinate for at least 20 minutes.

2. Rinse broccoli and place in a nonreactive bowl. Place a wet paper towel on top, then microwave for 2 minutes. Set aside.

3. Stir oyster sauce, water, 1 tablespoon Chinese rice wine, brown sugar, soy sauce, and remaining cornstarch in a bowl until well mixed. Set aside.

4. Heat wok over high heat. You want the wok to be very hot. Then, heat canola and sesame oil in wok and wait to become hot.

5. Working in batches, add steak and cook over high heat for 1 minute. Flip, and cook other side for another 1 minute. Transfer to a plate.

6. To the same wok, add garlic and ginger. Sauté for about 10 to 15 seconds then return beef to wok. Toss in heated

broccoli. Slightly stir prepared sauce to make sure cornstarch is not settled on the bottom, then add to wok. Toss everything in the sauce to combine. Continue cooking until sauce becomes thick.

7.   Garnish with sesame seeds. Serve.

Nutrition:

- Calories: 140

- Fat: 8g

- Carbs: 30

- Sugars: 10g

- Protein: 25g

Red Lobster's Shrimp Quiche

Preparation Time: 30 minutes

Cooking Time: 1 hour

Servings: 4–6

Ingredients:

- 1–9 inch Pre-baked pie crust

- 4 ounces Petite Alaskan shrimp

- ½cup grated Gruyere cheese

- 2 Whisked eggs

- 1 cup light sour cream

- 1 tablespoon green onions/chives

- Black pepper and salt

Directions:

1. Devein, cook, and peel the shrimp.

2. Warm the oven to 350° Fahrenheit.

3. Sprinkle the shrimp over the pie crust, adding the grated cheese.

4.   Finely chop the chives or onions. Combine the eggs, pepper, salt, sour cream, and green onions.

5.   Pour the mixture into the pie crust.

6.   Bake for 25 to 30 minutes.

7.   Serve warm or chilled.

Nutrition:

*   Calories: 112

*   Fat: 17

*   Carbs: 50g

*   Sugars: 5g

*   Protein: 7g

Cracker Barrel's Chicken Fried Chicken

Preparation Time: 15 minutes

Cooking Time: 30 minutes

Servings: 4

Ingredients:

- Chicken

- ½ cup all-purpose flour

- 1 teaspoon poultry seasoning

- ½ teaspoon salt

- ½ teaspoon pepper

- 1 egg, slightly beaten

- 1 tablespoon water

- 4 chicken breasts, pounded to a ½-inch thickness

- 1 cup vegetable oil

Gravy:

- 2 tablespoons all-purpose flour

- ¼ teaspoon salt

- ¼ teaspoon pepper

- 1¼ cups milk

Directions:

1.   Preheat the oven to 200°F.

2.   Mix the poultry seasoning, flour, salt, and pepper.

3.   In another shallow dish, mix the beaten egg and water.

4.   Coat both of the sides of the chicken breasts in the flour mixture, then dip them in the egg mixture. After this, coat it back into the flour mixture.

5.   Heat the vegetable oil over medium-high heat in a large deep skillet. A cast iron is a good choice if you have one. Put the chicken and cook for 15 minutes, or until fully cooked, turning over about halfway through.

6.   Place the chicken to a baking sheet and place in the oven to maintain temperature.

7.   Remove all but 2 tablespoons of oil from the skillet you cooked the chicken in.

8.   Prepare the gravy by whisking the dry gravy ingredients together in a bowl. Then whisk them into the oil in the skillet, stirring thoroughly to remove lumps. When the flour begins to brown, slowly whisk in the milk for about 2 minutes or until the mixture thickens.

9.   Top chicken with some of the gravy.

Nutrition:

- Calories: 242.8

- Fat: 6.6g

- Carbs: 38.4g

- Sugars: 3g

- Protein: 8.4g

Cracker Barrel's Chicken and Dumplings

Preparation Time: 30 minutes

Cooking Time: 20 minutes

Servings: 4

Ingredients:

- 2 cups flour

- ½ teaspoon baking powder

- 1 pinch salt

- 2 tablespoons butter

- 1 scant cup buttermilk

- 2 quarts chicken broth

- 3 cups cooked chicken

Directions:

1. Mix together in a bowl the salt, flour, and baking powder in a large bowl to make the dumplings. Cut the butter into the flour mixture. Pour in the milk slowly until it forms a dough ball.

2.	Cover your countertop with enough flour that the dough will not stick when you roll it out. Roll out the dough relatively thin, then cut into squares to form dumplings.

3.	Flour a plate and transfer the dough from the counter to the plate.

4.	Bring the chicken broth to a boil in a large saucepan, then drop the dumplings in one by one, stirring continually. The excess flour will thicken the broth. Cook it for 20-25 minutes or until the dumplings are no longer doughy.

5.	Add the chicken, stir to combine, and serve.

Nutrition:

- Calories: 115

- Fat: 14g

- Carbs: 78g

- Sugars: 9g

- Protein: 8g

Chipotle's California Grilled Chicken

Preparation time: 35 minutes

Cooking time: 20 minutes

Servings: 4

Ingredients:

- 4 boneless, skinless chicken breasts

- 3/4 cup balsamic vinegar

- 2 tablespoons extra virgin olive oil

- 1 tablespoon honey

- 1 teaspoon oregano

- 1 teaspoon basil

- 1 teaspoon garlic powder

For garnish:

- Sea salt

- Black pepper, fresh ground

- 4 slices fresh mozzarella cheese

- 4 slices avocado

- 4 slices beefsteak tomato

- Balsamic glaze, for drizzling

Directions:

1.   Mix the balsamic vinegar, honey, olive oil, oregano, basil and garlic powder in a large mixing bowl.

2.   Add chicken to coat and marinate for 30 minutes in the refrigerator.

3.   Preheat grill and cook the chicken for 7 minutes each side.

4.   Top each chicken breast with mozzarella, avocado, and tomato and tent with foil on the grill to melt for 2 minutes.

5.   Drizzle some of balsamic glaze, and a pinch of sea salt and black pepper.

Nutrition:

•   Calories: 883

•   Sugar: 15.2g

•   Fat: 62.1g

•   Carbs: 29.8g

•   Protein: 55.3g

Chipotle's Salsa Verde Marinated Chicken

Preparation time: 4 hours 35 minutes

Cooking time: 4 hours 50 minutes

Servings: 6

Ingredients:

- 6 boneless, skinless chicken breasts
- 1 tablespoon olive oil
- 1 teaspoon sea salt
- 1 teaspoon chili powder
- 1 teaspoon ground cumin
- 1 teaspoon garlic powder
- For the salsa Verde marinade:
- 3 teaspoons garlic, minced
- 1 small onion, chopped
- 6 tomatillos, husked, rinsed and chopped
- 1 medium jalapeño pepper, cut in half, seeded
- ¼ cup fresh cilantro, chopped
- ½ teaspoon sugar or sugar substitute

Directions:

1.   Add salsa Verde marinade Ingredients to a food processor and pulse until smooth. Mix sea salt, chili powder, cumin, and garlic powder together in a small mixing bowl. Season the chicken with olive oil and seasoning mix, and lay in glass baking dish. Spread a tablespoon of salsa Verde marinade over each chicken breast to cover; reserve remaining salsa for serving. Refrigerate for 4 hours. Brush some olive oil on the griller and preheat. Add the chicken to the grill and cook 7 minutes per. Serve each with additional salsa Verde and enjoy!

Nutrition:

- Calories: 321

- Sugar: 1.3g

- Fat: 13.7g

- Carbs: 4.8g

- Protein: 43g

PASTA, SOUP & VEGETABLES

Denny's Broccoli Cheese Soup

Preparation Time: 5 minutes

Cooking Time: 1 hour 10 minutes

Servings: 4

Ingredients:

- ⅛ teaspoon of white pepper

- ¼ teaspoon of salt

- 4 cups chopped broccoli florets

- 2 ¼ cups chicken broth

- 3 cups shredded mild cheddar cheese

- 1 ½ cups whole milk

- ¼ cup all-purpose flour

- ¼ cup butter

Directions:

1.   Let the butter melt in medium heat then add the flour and cook for about 1 minute, while stirring constantly.

2.   Prepare a roux by whisking some milk in the saucepan, adding some cheese to it, and stirring until the cheese has melted.

3.   Add the remaining ingredients, stir them all together and continue cooking until the soup boils. Let it simmer in low heat for 60 minutes while stirring often. Make sure the broccoli is tender before serving.

Nutrition:

- Calories: 324

- Fat: 23g

- Carbs: 26g

- Protein: 31g

KFC's Coleslaw

Preparation Time: 15 minutes

Cooking Time: 0 minutes

Servings: 10

Ingredients:

- 8 cups cabbage, finely diced
- ¼ cup carrot, finely diced
- 2 tablespoons onions, minced
- ⅓ cup granulated sugar
- ½ teaspoon salt
- ⅛ Teaspoon pepper
- ¼ cup milk
- ½ cup mayonnaise
- ¼ cup buttermilk
- 1½ tablespoons white vinegar
- 2½ tablespoons lemon juice

Directions:

1. Combine the cabbage, carrot, and onions in a bowl.

2.   Place the rest of the ingredients in a blender or food processor and blend until smooth. Pour the sauce over the cabbage mixture.

3.   Put inside the refrigerator for several hours before serving.

Nutrition:

- Calories 49.6

- Total Fat 0.3 g

- Carbs 11.3 g

- Protein 1.2 g

- Sodium 138.3 mg

Mediterranean's Italian Pasta

Preparation Time: 10 minutes

Cooking Time: 30 minutes

Servings: 4

Ingredients:

- 3 anchovies

- 9 ounces mozzarella cheese

- 13 ounces whole-wheat pasta

- 2 tablespoon olives

- 3 tomatoes

- 3 tablespoon olive oil

- Pepper

- Salt

Directions:

1. Cook the pasta in boiling water.

2. Meanwhile chop the tomatoes, the mozzarella, and the anchovies.

3. Once the pasta is cooked, use some cold water to cool it.

4.   Season with the chop ingredients, add the olive oil, some salt, pepper, and basil.

Nutrition:

- Calories: 100

- Protein: 8g

- Carbohydrate: 18g

- Fat: 6g

Mediterranean's Gricia Spaghetti

Preparation Time: 15 minutes

Cooking Time: 30 minutes

Servings: 4

Ingredients:

- 13 ounces whole wheat spaghetti
- 5 ounces pork cheek
- 2 ounces roman pecorino
- Salt

Directions:

1. Cut the pork cheek in ⅓ inches strips.

2. In a pan, cook the pork cheek over medium heat for 10 minutes.

3. Meanwhile, cook the spaghetti in salted boiling water.

4. When the spaghetti pasta is cooked, drain it and pour it in the pork cheek pan. Add the roman pecorino and mix everything.

Nutrition:

- Calories: 110

- Protein: 10g

- Carbohydrate: 28g

- Fat: 7g

Mediterranean's Zucchini Carbonara Pasta

Preparation Time: 15 minutes

Cooking Time: 25 minutes

Servings: 4

Ingredients:

- 13 ounces whole-wheat pasta

- 2 eggs

- 2 tablespoon olive oil

- 2 zucchini

- 1 garlic clove

- 2 tablespoon milk

- Salt

- Parmesan

Directions:

1.   Cut the zucchinis into small pieces. Put olive oil in a pan to let it heat and add the garlic clove. After a few minutes add the zucchinis and cook for 10 minutes.

2.   Cook the pasta in boiling water, meanwhile beat the

eggs together with the milk in a big bowl. Add the parmesan

and some salt.

3.   If the pasta is cooked already, drain it and add it into

the pan. Pour the pan content into the bowl and mix

everything.

Nutrition:

•   Calories: 105

•   Protein: 10g

•   Carbohydrate: 23g

•   Fat: 9g

Olive Garden's Chicken and Gnocchi Soup

Preparation Time: 30 minutes

Cooking Time: 30 minutes

Servings: 6

Ingredients:

- ¼ cup butter

- 1 tablespoon extra-virgin olive oil

- 1 large zucchini, chopped

- 2 stalks celery, chopped

- 1 yellow onion, chopped

- ½ red bell pepper, chopped

- 2 carrots, grated

- 4 garlic cloves, finely chopped

- ¼ cup all-purpose flour

- 3 cups chicken broth

- 3 cups half-and-half

- 2 cups rotisserie chicken meat, shredded

- 1 (16-ounce) package small gnocchi

- 2 cups fresh spinach, chopped

- Salt and pepper, to taste

- ½ teaspoon ground thyme

- ¼ teaspoon nutmeg, grated

Directions:

1. Heat butter together with olive oil on medium heat. Add zucchini, celery, onion, red bell pepper, carrots, and garlic. Sauté for about 8 to 10 minutes until tender, then mix in flour to coat vegetables. Cook for another 2 minutes.

2. Pour chicken broth in pot and stir for 5 minutes until ingredients are combined and soup is smooth and has thickened. Then, stir in half-and-half and cook for another 5 minutes until soup is a bit thicker. Slowly stir in chicken, gnocchi, and spinach. Sprinkle in salt, pepper, thyme, and nutmeg.

3. Serve.

Nutrition:

- Calories: 416

- Total Fat: 24g

- Carbs: 35g

- Sugar: 8g

- Fibers: 3g

- Protein: 17g

Applebees's Tomato Basil Soup

Preparation Time: 10 minutes

Cooking Time: 20 minutes

Servings: 8

Ingredients:

- 3 tablespoons olive oil

- 1 small garlic clove, finely chopped

- 1 (10 ¾-ounce) can condensed tomato soup

- ¼ cup bottled marinara sauce

- 5 ounces water

- 1 teaspoon fresh oregano, diced

- ½ teaspoon ground black pepper

- 1 tablespoon fresh basil, diced

- 6 Italian-style seasoned croutons

- 2 tablespoons Parmesan cheese, shredded

Directions:

1. Put oil in a medium sized pan over medium heat. Add garlic and stir fry for 2 to 3 minutes or until garlic is soft and aromatic.

2.   Pour tomato soup and marinara sauce into pan and stir. Add water gradually. Toss in oregano and pepper. Once simmering, reduce heat to low. Cook for 15 minutes until all the flavors are combined. Add basil and stir.

3.   Transfer to bowls. Add croutons on top and sprinkle with Parmesan cheese.

4.   Serve.

Nutrition:

• Calories 350

• Total fat 26g

• Carbs 28g

• Sugar 14g

• Protein 6g

Panera's Lemon Chicken Orzo Soup

Preparation Time: 10 minutes

Cooking Time: 1 hour

Servings: 12

Ingredients:

- Water, for boiling

- Salt, to taste

- 8 ounces orzo pasta

- 1 teaspoon olive oil

- 3 carrots, diced

- 3 ribs celery, diced

- 1 onion, diced

- 2 cloves garlic, finely chopped

- ½ teaspoon dried thyme

- ½ teaspoon dried oregano

- Salt, to taste

- Pepper, to taste

- 1 bay leaf

- 3 (32-ounce) cartons chicken broth

- ½ cup fresh lemon juice

- 1 lemon, zested

- 8 ounces cooked chicken breast, diced

- 1 (8-ounce) package baby spinach leaves

- 1 lemon, sliced

- ¼ cup Parmesan cheese, shredded

Directions:

1. Pour water and add a pinch of salt to a pot and bring to a boil and put the orzo and cook until pasta is al dente. Remove from heat and drain.

2. Put olive oil in medium heat. Add carrots, celery, and onion. Sauté for about 5 to 7 minutes until vegetables become tender and onion is translucent. Stir in garlic. Cook for another minute or until aromatic. Toss in the thyme, oregano, salt, black pepper, and bay leaf. Add chicken broth. Bring to a boil.

3. Bring heat to medium-low. Let it simmer for 10 minutes.

4. Add orzo and lemon zest. Pour in lemon juice and the chicken. Cook everything for about 3 minutes until both the chicken and orzo are heated thoroughly. Toss in spinach and

cook for about 2 to 3 minutes. The soup is ready once the spinach wilts into the broth and the orzo is soft.

5.   Transfer into bowls and serve with lemon slices and Parmesan cheese.

Nutrition:

- Calories: 167
- Total Fat: 4g
- Carbs: 22g
- Sugar: 4g
- Protein 12g
- Sodium 187 mg

SNACKS & DESSERTS

Taco Bells's Grilled Steak Soft Tacos

Preparation Time: 10 minutes

Cooking Time: 20 minutes

Servings: 6

Ingredients:

The Salsa:

- 2 large tomatoes
- ½ cup red onion
- ¼ cup lime juice
- 1 Jalapeno pepper
- 3 tablespoon fresh cilantro
- ⅓ teaspoons salt, divided
- 2 teaspoons ground cumin, divided
- 1.5 lb. beef flank steak
- 1 tablespoon canola oil
- 6 @ 8 inches whole wheat tortillas
- 1 onion
- Optional: lime wedges & sliced avocado

Directions:

1.   Deseed and chop the tomatoes and jalapeno. Dice the onion and cilantro.

2.   Combine the first five fixings (before the line). Stir in one teaspoon cumin and ¼ teaspoon salt. Set it to the side for now.

3.   Sprinkle the steak using the rest of the salt and cumin.

4.   Grill using the medium temperature setting (with a lid on) until the meat is as you like it (med-rare, on an instant-read thermometer, is about 135°F), or 6–8 minutes. Let the cooked meat stand for 5 minutes before slicing.

5.   Warm the oil in a skillet using the med-high temperature setting and sauté them until the onion is crisp-tender.

6.   Slice steak thinly across the grain and serve on tortillas with onion and salsa.

7.   If desired, serve with avocado and lime wedges.

Nutrition:

•   Calories: 329

- Protein: 27g

- Fat: 12g

- Carbohydrates: 29g

- Sugars: 3g

Mesa Grill's Honey Glazed Salmon

Preparation Time: 15 minutes

Cooking Time: 40 minutes

Servings: 4

Ingredients:

- 4 pieces salmon steaks

- 3 tablespoons olive oil

- 5 tablespoon lemon juice

- 2 tablespoon balsamic vinegar

- 3 pieces garlic cloves

- 1 tablespoon ginger root

- 2 bunch cilantro

- 4 tablespoon honey

- 2 tablespoon mustard

Directions:

1.	Mix 2 tablespoons of olive oil, lemon juice, balsamic vinegar, chopped garlic, ginger, and cilantro (set aside 3 tablespoons of greens). Marinate the fish in the resulting mixture for 1–2 hours.

2.   For the glaze, mix honey, mustard, leftover olive oil, and cilantro. Preheat the oven in grill mode.

3.   Cook the fish in the oven for 8-9 minutes, periodically pouring marinade. A few minutes before the end of cooking, grease the fish on both sides with icing. It should turn into a crust, but not burn.

4.   On the side, grilled vegetables and a glass of chilled white wine are perfect. Serve and enjoy!

Nutrition:

- Calories: 150

- Fat: 4.2g

- Carbs: 40g

- Sugars: 1g

- Protein: 9g

El Ranchoro's Grande Baja Fish Tacos

Preparation Time: 10 minutes

Cooking Time: 20 minutes

Servings: 5

Ingredients:

- ½ cup (125 ml) mayonnaise

- 2 c. (30 ml) water

- 1 Restaurant Baja Fish Soft Taco Set

- 400g white fish fillets, thawed if frozen (about ¾ to 1 lb.)

- Suggested garnishes: finely grated cabbage, fresh coriander, a touch of lemon or lime juice

Directions:

1. Mix the contents of the seasoning bag for Baja sauce (all) with mayonnaise and water until well blended; Reserve.

2. Pour the contents of the fish seasoning packet (from the set) into a shallow dish or bowl. If the fish is dry, wet it lightly with a damp paper towel. Place the fish fillets on the

seasoning, then turn them so that they are very lightly coated on both sides.

3.   Light the barbecue with gas or charcoal. Before cooking the fish, while the grill is clean, grill the soft flour tortillas (from the set) directly on the grill for 15 to 20 seconds on each side (or until they are lightly browned and toasted); wrap the tortillas in aluminum foil to keep them warm until ready to assemble.

4.   Brush the grill with vegetable oil or use a grill basket for the fish (generously coat the basket with cooking spray or brush with oil). Grill the fish over medium-high heat for 3 to 4 minutes on each side (note: thicker fish fillets may require more cooking time). Remove it from the griller and let it sit for 4 to 5 minutes.

5.   Divide the fish into 10 portions and divide over the hot and toasted tortillas. Add grated cabbage, Baja sauce, and cilantro and squeeze a little lemon or lime juice over it.

Nutrition:

• Calories: 100

• Fat: 3g

- Carbs: 21g

- Sugars: 10g

- Protein: 5g

Taco Bells's Delicious Tacos

Preparation Time: 10 minutes

Cooking Time: 20 minutes

Servings: 12

Ingredients:

- 1 ½ tablespoon golden MasaHarina corn flour, ex.

Bob's Red Mill

- 1.33 lb. ground chuck

- 4-5 teaspoons chili powder

- ¼ teaspoons sugar

- ¼ teaspoons ground cumin

- 1 teaspoons dried minced onion

- 5 teaspoons spices

- Onion powder

- Seasoning salt

- Garlic powder

- Paprika

- Garlic salt

- Beef bouillon powder

To Serve:

- 12 taco shells

- Shredded Iceberg lettuce

- 2 Diced Roma tomatoes

- 1 cup shredded cheddar cheese

- Optional: Sour cream

Directions:

2.   Combine all of the 'beef filling' fixings except for the meat. Combine the spice mix - blending thoroughly.

3.   Cook the beef until browned. Transfer it from the burner and dump the meat into a strainer to rinse with hot water.

4.   Toss the beef into the pan and stir in the spice mix with water (75–1 cup). Simmer using the med-low temperature setting to cook away most of the liquids (20 min.)

5.   Prepare the tacos. Pop the shells into a 350° Fahrenheit oven for 7–10 minutes.

6.   Assemble them with the meat, lettuce, tomatoes, sour cream, and cheese to your liking.

7.   Serve them promptly.

Nutrition:

- Calories: 236

- Protein: 12g

- Fat: 15g

- Carbohydrates: 10g

- Sugars: 1g

Chili's Spicy Shrimp Tacos

Preparation Time: 10 minutes

Cooking Time: 15 minutes

Servings: 6

Ingredients:

- 500g fresh shrimp, clean

- 1 tablespoons butter

- Sea salt to taste

- 1 ½ cups refried beans

- 6 large flour tortillas

- 1 sliced avocado

For the coriander mayonnaise:

- 1 yolk

- 1 medium garlic clove, coarsely minced

- 1 Serrano pepper, deveined and coarsely chopped

- ¾ cup olive oil

- 1 large bunch coriander leaves (about 1 ½ cups leaves)

- 2 to 3 tablespoons of lemon juice

Directions:

1.   Prepare the mayonnaise first. In the blender, place the egg yolk with the minced garlic. Add the olive oil in a fine trickle little by little. Add the serrano pepper and increase the speed to medium. Gradually add the coriander leaves and finish with the lemon juice (add 2 or 3 tablespoon as needed). Finish seasoning with sea salt to taste.

2.   Cover with plastic wrap. If prepared in advance, keep in the fridge.

3.   Heat a large, low skillet over medium-high heat. Add a tablespoon of butter and sauté half the shrimp with a little salt until they are pink and firm. Remove from heat immediately.

4.   Simultaneously heat tortillas and beans to serve: on each tortilla, add two tablespoons of beans, continue with the shrimp, two slices avocado and finish generously with mayonnaise.

Nutrition:

- Calories: 242.8
- Fat: 6.6g
- Carbs: 38.4g

- Sugars: 3g

- Protein: 8.4g

Red Lobster's Cheddar Bay Biscuits

Preparation Time: 10 minutes

Cooking Time: 15 minutes

Servings: 14

Ingredients:

- 1 tablespoon granulated sugar

- 2 cups all-purpose flour (2 cups)

- 1 teaspoons kosher salt

- 1 tablespoon baking powder

- 1 tablespoon garlic powder

- 8 tablespoon melted unsalted butter, divided

- 1 cup whole milk

- 8 ounces shredded Mild cheddar cheese

Directions:

1.   Heat the oven at 400° Fahrenheit. Cover a baking tray using a sheet of parchment baking paper.

2.   Sift the garlic powder, ½ teaspoon of salt, flour, baking powder, and sugar into a hefty-sized mixing container.

3.   Melt one stick of butter with the milk and cheddar cheese - don't over mix.

4.   Drop 14 biscuits onto the prepared baking sheet. Bake until the biscuits are browned (10−12 min.)

5.   Mix the remaining butter, salt, and parsley to brush the tops of the biscuits before serving.

Nutrition:

- Calories: 140

- Fat: 8g

- Carbs: 30

- Sugars: 10g

- Protein: 25g

York's Peppermint Patties

Preparation Time: 15 minutes

Cooking Time: 40 minutes

Servings: 5

Ingredients:

*   14 ounces Condensed Milk

*   1 tablespoon peppermint extricate green or red food
shading, discretionary

*   6 cups confectioners' sugar

*   1-16 ounces sack semi–sweet chocolate chips

Directions:

1.   In a huge blender bowl, consolidate Eagle Brand,
concentrate, and food shading whenever wanted. Include 6
cups sugar; beat on low speed until smooth and very much
mixed. Turn blend onto a surface sprinkled with confectioners'
sugar.

2.   Massage gently to frame smooth ball. Shape into 1–inch balls. Spot 2 inches separated on wax paper–lined preparing sheets. Level each ball into a ½ inch patty. Let dry 1 hour or more.

3.   Liquefy the chocolate contributes a microwave set on high for 2 minutes. Mix part of the way through the warming time. Dissolve completely, however, don't overheat. Dissolving the chocolate chips should likewise be possible utilizing a double–boiler over low warmth. With a fork, plunges every patty into warm chocolate.

Nutrition:

*   Calories: 140

*   Fat: 8g

*   Carbs: 30

*   Sugars: 10g

*   Protein: 25g

Starbucks'Cinnamon Rolls

Preparation Time: 20 minutes

Cooking Time: 30 minutes

Servings: 8

Ingredients:

Batter:

- 2 packs dry yeast

- Half cup warm water

- ⅓ cup sugar

- ½ teaspoon sugar

- 4–5 cups all–purpose flour,

- 1 teaspoon salt

- 1 cup milk, singed and cooled to 110 degrees

- ⅓ cup vegetable oil

- 2 eggs,

- ½ cup butter or margarine, Full

- 1 cup colored sugar

- 2 tablespoons cinnamon Icing:

- 1 cup confectioners' sugar

- 2–3 tablespoons warm milk

- 1 teaspoon vanilla

Directions:

1. For the batter, break down yeast in water with ½ teaspoon sugar. Let stand for 5 minutes. In blending bowl, join 3 cups flour, ⅓ cup sugar, and salt. At low speed, progressively beat in milk, oil, eggs, and yeast blend; beat until all-around mixed. Beat in extra flour until batter pulls from sides of the bowl.

2. On a floured surface, massage batter until smooth and versatile, 8–10 minutes. A spot in a lubed bowl, going to oil top. Spread and let ascend in the warm, draft–free territory until multiplied in mass, around 60 minutes.

3. For the filling, beat all fixings together until smooth.

4. Put in a safe spot. Oil 2 (9–inch) round cake skillet. On a daintily floured surface, fold batter into an 18 X 10-inch square shape. Spread with filling. Roll firmly from the long side. Cut into 14 (¼–inch) cuts. Spot 1 move cut side up in the focus of each dish. Orchestrate

5.   Spread and let ascend until multiplied in mass, 30 to 40 minutes. Preheat stove to 350°C. Prepare 25 to 30 minutes, until brilliant earthy colored. Cool in skillet 10 minutes.

6.   For the icing, whisk all fixings until smooth.

Nutrition:

- Calories: 160

- Fat: 10g

- Carbs: 50g

- Sugars: 6g

- Protein: 12g

Taco Bells's Chalupa Supreme

Preparation Time: 15 minutes

Cooking Time: 20 minutes

Servings: 6

Ingredients:

- 6 @ 6 inches Corn tortillas

- 2 teaspoons olive oil

- ⅓ cup Shredded part-skim mozzarella cheese

- 2 cups Cooked chicken breast

- Diced tomatoes with green chiles

- 1 teaspoons ground cumin

- 1 teaspoons garlic powder

- ¼ teaspoons black pepper and salt

- 1 teaspoons Onion powder

- ½ cup finely shredded cabbage

Directions:

1. Warm the oven in advance at 350°F. Arrange the tortillas on an ungreased baking sheet. Brush them using a bit of oil and a sprinkle of cheese.

2.   Chop and toss the chicken, tomatoes, and seasonings in a large skillet. Simmer and stir using the medium temperature setting (6–8 min.) or until most of the liquid is evaporated.

3.   Spoon the delicious mixture over the tortillas.

4.   Bake it for 15–18 minutes until the tortillas are crisp and cheese is melted. Garnish with the cabbage.

Nutrition:

- Calories: 206

- Carbohydrates: 17g

- Protein: 19g

- Fat: 6g

- Sugars: 3g

DRINKS

Olive Garden's Watermelon Moscato Sangria

Preparation Time: 7 minutes

Cooking Time: 0 minutes

Servings: 6

Ingredients:

- 4 cups Ice

- 750ml. Moscato

- 1 orange (sliced)

- 6 ounces each of:

- Watermelon syrup

- Ginger ale

- ¾ cup strawberries (sliced)

Directions:

1. Wash the fruits and make small-sized slices by cutting them.

2. Use a large-sized pitcher for pouring the moscato.

3.   Mix watermelon syrup and ginger ale in the pitcher and stir them for mixing completely.

4.   Stir the mixture slowly within the pitcher after the mixing ice.

5.   Then, combine sliced strawberries and oranges in the mixture.

6.   As per your choice, serve the drink with sliced watermelon.

Nutrition:

- Calories: 204
- Protein: 0g
- Fat: 0g
- Carbs: 33g
- Fiber: 0g

Los Cabos' Mexican Spiked Coffee

Preparation Time: 5 minutes

Cooking Time: 0 minutes

Servings: 1

Ingredients:

- 1 ounces Tequila Blanco
- ½ ounces Kahlua
- 6 ounces Black coffee
- Whipped cream
- Cinnamon powder
- Sugar

Directions:

1. Wet the edge of the glass in water and coat with the sugar.

2. Caramelize the sugar rim.

3. Flame the tequila & Kahlua and serve in a glass with the sugar rim.

4. After that, add black coffee and whipped cream, and then top with cinnamon.

Nutrition:

- Calories: 120

- Fat: 15g

- Carbs: 45g

- Sugar: 8g

- Protein: 14g

Sonic Drive-in's Strawberry Shake

Preparation Time: 5 minutes

Cooking Time: 0 minutes

Servings: 2

Ingredients:

- 1 ½ ice cream (vanilla)

- 1 tablespoon strawberry preserves

- ⅓ cup 2% milk

- ½ of frozen strawberries (unsweetened)

Directions:

1. Take all the ingredients in a blender and make a smooth mixture.

2.   Serve it to enjoy immediately by pouring them in chilled glasses.

Nutrition:

- Calories: 257
- Protein: 5g
- Fat: 12g
- Carbs: 35g
- Fiber: 1g

Starbucks' Pink Drink

Preparation Time: 30 minutes

Cooking Time: 0 minutes

Servings: 2

Ingredients:

- 1–2 cups coconut milk (Unsweetened)
- 1 cup hot boiling water
- Strawberries (fresh and sliced)
- ½ cup grape juice (white)
- 4 packs of acai berry tea

Optional:

- Agave nectar

Directions:

1. Use two cups measuring glass for placing acai berry teas after unwrapping them. Mix hot water in it and leave it to cool down it. Toss the tea packets after squeezing them.

2. Combine grape juice in the prepared tea within the measuring cup.

3. Use ice and one cup tea mixture for filling a cup.

4. Also, use coconut milk as per your choice for the toppings of the drink.

5. You can use slices strawberries and any type of sweetener as per your choice.

6. Serve and enjoy!

Nutrition:

- Calories: 124
- Protein: 2g
- Fat: 5g
- Carbs: 21g
- Fiber: 2g

Smoothie King's Caribbean Way

Preparation Time: 5 minutes

Cooking Time: 0 minutes

Servings: 2

Ingredients:

- 1 cup papaya nectar

- 1 banana (average)

- 1 ½ cups ice

- 2 cups strawberries (fresh)

- ¼ cup turbinado sugar

Directions:

1. Use a blender for mixing papaya nectar, banana, strawberries, and sugar and make a puree after covering it.

2. Make a smooth mixture by adding ice to the prepared puree.

3. Enjoy it after serving.

Nutrition:

- Calories: 261

- Protein: 2g

- Fat: 1g

- Carbs: 65g

- Fiber: 5g

Panera's Mango Smoothie

Preparation Time: 10 minutes

Cooking Time: 0 minutes

Servings: 2

Ingredients:

- ½ banana (medium ripe))

- 1 tablespoon honey

- ½ cup each of:

- Pineapple juice (unsweetened)

- Plain yogurt (reduced fat)

- 2 cups frozen mango (chopped after peeling)

Directions:

1.   Mix all the ingredients using a blender and make a smooth mixture.

2.   Serve it immediately after pouring the smoothie in chilled glasses.

Nutrition:

- Calories: 237

- Protein: 5g

- Fat: 2g

- Carbs: 56g

- Fiber: 4g

CPSIA information can be obtained
at www.ICGtesting.com
Printed in the USA
BVHW051053070421
604208BV00019B/518